£ 3

That Water Speaks in Tongues

Siobhán Campbell

Templar Poetry

First Published 2008 by Templar Poetry
Templar Poetry is an imprint of Delamide & Bell

Fenelon House,
Kingsbridge Terrace
Dale Road, Matlock, Derbyshire
DE4 3NB

www.templarpoetry.co.uk

ISBN 978-1-906285-23-4

For permission to reprint or broadcast these poems write to
Templar Poetry

Typeset by Pliny
Graphics by Paloma Violet
Printed and bound in Turkey

for Amy, Luke and Eoin

Acknowledgements

Acknowledgments are made to the editors of the following journals in which some of these poems appeared: *Magma, Poetry* (Chicago), *The Southern Review* (Louisiana), *Wasafiri Magazine, Cyphers, Crannóg, Brand, Poetry Ireland Review, Oxford Magazine.* 'Platform' was commended in the National Poetry Competition, 2005. 'These Women' was awarded second place in the 2007 Troubadour International poetry competition. 'When I Asked my Dad About Warrenpoint' won an award in the Wigtown Booktown ScotlandPoetry Competition 2008. 'Quickthorn' was recorded as 'The Hawthorn Bush' on *Lifelines2* poetry cd, Oxfam Books and Music 2007.

Contents

Quickthorn

Don't bring haw into the house at night
or in any month with a red fruit in season
or when starlings bank against the light,
don't bring haw in. Don't give me reason
to think you have hidden haw about you.
Tucked in secret, may its thorn thwart you.
Plucked in blossom, powdered by your thumb,
I will smell it for the hum of haw is long,
its hold is low and lilting. If you bring
haw in, I will know you want me gone
to the fairies and their jilting. I will know
you want me buried in the deep green field
where god knows what is rotting.

Will of the People

If, in the many-spangled cheek of a high wire walker,
the print of a footstep edges toward her pretty ear;
if she is used by the elephant act before the interval
while out back the hippo is hosed down to keep him cool
and in the tent this lumbering creaser is approaching
her small white cheek and the fool signals the foot to fall –
Elephant keeper, how could you let it happen?
How could you take us to the brink of ourselves,
knowing that we make her fly through our sparked clapping,
how we swing our emotional track when she runs the wire?
We could nearly have cried if the moment became a story.
Given all this, that it is ruined, will we return, chanting slogans
about cruelty, root you off that green we laid near the parks?

Prime

There was a way to live from hand to mouth
and you wiped the mouth too, from the corners
in case anything was missed.
Your apron caught the crumbs of soda bread
each lifted by finger and thumb, made round
on the way to your tongue.
The burst seeds of a tomato, its pitted juice
scooped with a spoon, rapid with salt.
The bone of a lamb leg with a white hinge
at the joint, its centre packed with black marrow.
What sweetness, like plenty from heaven.
As if this is what makes everything move.

Rosé

The rose that leaves fat hips after the bloom
is not the rose the gardener loves to love
until her thrift-reared neighbour from the north
helps her harvest them for rose-hip syrup.
Good for colds, for any ailments of the blood,
to rub on creaky joints and boost the bowels.
You'll have the old women in when they hear
that you've sugared your hips, she's told.
The gardener, who knows how these things go,
is sure that they'd prefer to wet their lips.

Blind Eye

Beware the man who ploughed a fairy ring.
He wouldn't be stopped by tale or deed
though moss fell off his roof in clumps
and starlings abandoned his haggart.

He hoped the cypress would not see,
by the strobe light high on his tractor,
how the whites of his eyes had already pooled
with things you can tell no neighbour.

He kept china dogs on his mantle,
one had a painted monocle;
Three monkeys down by the hearth
gathered to say no evil.

He never thought of the roots of trees
stalled in their reaching mirror,
the desperate effort of their shift
as diesel fumes came nearer.

Beware the man who forgets,
who sees his wheat ripen like gangrene
the best of it splayed in a patch of flat
that others swear is a ring.

Platform

'My mother's yard was the cleanest one in Templeboy,'
the station master said as we waited for the ten eleven.
'In her haggart you could see the snips of granite glisten
like the promise of confetti shining up as you went by.
No rat ever darkened the door of her feed shed either
and as for the cattle, if they were in, she was after them
with a mop. She'd have yard trained them if we'd let her.

There was one dip where a puddle settled, a filthy mirror.
She drove herself mad over how to be rid of that water.
How could she brush it away without making a muck?
She would nearly have sucked it up with the hoover
when she thought of the dog. The dog that needed
to drink or else be starved. So after rain, she brought
that mutt to water, finished off the job with lemon cleaner.'

Now, you may think there was only him and me involved
in our encounter before the train arrived. But I could swear
I heard the muttering of another streel behind him as he ran
to wave his flag and that surely was the sound of something
parched that carped the distance just as I embarked.

Canola

Far from the astronomers and the counsellors,
the princess gathers her most loyal courtiers
to the safe landing-place for underlings.

If we arrange ourselves like this, she says,
bending her supple back to reveal the lemon suns,
we will survive the collapse of everything we know.

Her maids try the pose, decide it's surprisingly comfortable.
'In the coming times there will be travellers
who'll look from their windows past the subtle greens

stunned by our parade of brightest yellow.
Rape they will say, knowingly, as the word turns
into something like oil on their tongue.'

These Women

'These men are no dreamers'
MacDiarmid , 'The Wreck of the Swan'

These women are no dreamers.
They make happen the full wake,
the kettle hopping, the oven warm.

They take death in hand
and force him to be civil.
In their lighting, the spitting candle calms
and the rosary settles out of irony.

These women are not kind
if you do not iron the sheets you borrowed,
if you bring batch instead of sliced,
what good is that for sandwiches?

These women bar all holds in the
screamed stall of the birthroom.
Instead they ask for the gummed grit
they found for themselves in that
most alone of coupled moments.

These women know how to mash potatoes
so that they charge despair
out of a teenager.

They have followed a father
and a small child on a combine harvester,
not to pick up the pieces of the boy's arm

and bring them to his mother,
but because they felt the call of the back field
like something rotting in the feed shed
before chief rat jumps out.

These women will not pass through
the horse meadow, even on a summer night,
for there they have felt that the world might let us go.

They've seen the consequence of that.
Ironing keeps it at bay
and doing what is right.

Giving the Talk

I know every stick and stone of this old road
every hollyhock and foxglove
where the flesh fly lays her eggs in devil spit;
which hedges harbour the blackthorn
and where to pick the best berries, high up
and low down. Like us all, round here,
I know which corner the articulated lorry
jackknifed, taking a shortcut off the main road,
scattering the limbs of the two Brady children
on either side. No-one put flowers
or one of those little crosses. Slowing down
on that bend, as everyone here knows,
is treacherous.

Pitched

Here, in our own time, a living memory
exists of a man who made nature out of mind.
A bent man, curved in a crook, who skewed
the ash trees, tied them down, flexed them
until the arc of his wishing came to be
and they reached toward their full becoming.
These were the unimaginable hayforks, all
of a piece, no maker's mark, a tine so precise
it made lifting two bales entirely possible.
Yes, they were for sale but at a price,
a different amount for every purchaser, a sum
to be reckoned after a month, their time
to coddle the sweep of the instrument in
newly worn hands, when they felt it sway
in the dip of one finger, and could watch
the wood seize their thumb print, its first knots
smoothed out of nodules. Put aside, laid down
and walked away from in a barn, or propped
in a rack, a branch might begin in a dint of work
and were it forgotten, left like a body in the dark
it might slip out a root. But this is conjecture.
What is certain is that these hayforks
would never warp once bent.

When All this is Over

I plan to go north
by unapproved roads
where sniper signs rust on the trees.

I will cross the border
over and back
several times to see how it feels.

I will dance the pig's dyke
and taste mountain mayflower
on the breeze.

Near under-fished lakes
I will hear a blood-pause
in the reach of the night

when every word used for batter
and crisis will cruise with the ease
of what runs right through us,

when the shift and fill
of my own dear cells
is all they will tell as they breathe.

And out through the lanes
I will lie in my form
in overgrown fields

not a chopper in sight,
when they say it is safe
and the weather agrees.

Sinister

it's not a right, it's a preference
to sit on the left side of the lord
swing down the sinistral and god I know it well
how to make ends meet, how to cut my cloth to suit my measure
wear the cuffs long so they might not see
the mark of the sinner
the troubles were never like this, Citóg
forced to write with your right
did you want to be saved or not
doing the work of the devil
and you could never hold a hurl right either
sure look at how you grip the knife
the way it would cut off more than you could chew
or blind the eye that is bigger than your stomach.

When I Asked my Dad about Warrenpoint

he said it was where folks gave up
grouse shooting and pheasant hunting for Lent,
where boys tongued it home with blackened mouths
after sucking the leaves of the aniseed bush
in the church grounds,
where once, at the dock dance, his sister
made him get back on the ferry without looking round
in case he would see his dead ringer.

She had given him, but not him, a jitterbug earlier,
her fright at the southern accent you could cut
and the look in his gamey eye.
She told Dad that he was the better looking, and she lied.
Still, it was best for the girls of two nations
that neither of them died.

Troubled

My father's foil,
A cousin once removed, signed up
For the Royal Irish Guards
Played rugby and deck quoits
On board a ship he built for
Workman Clark,
Drank gin with a twist
Voted for the Communists
Asked who carried on when Cain finished Abel,
Had it all to lose
Never wrote a word.

Or was he that other?
The one who turned
Fell for an Antrim princess
Pulled off a piece of causeway to keep,
Brought bad luck with it to the wains,
Smuggled petrol over the border
Cut growth hormone with talcum powder
Had three bulls in different fields
Developed a rare mini-marrow.

Crossing by Ferry

We try to heed the tiny signs
lodged behind his rheumy eyes,
how we are sized up for weight
as regulars file on in.
We had imagined tattooed arms
but couldn't stare to read.
The wallet at the back of his thigh
is packed with fares.
Is the woman in grey coming or going?
She coughs something up onto her chest
and leaves it there as an answer.

Out from shore the current knows
which waves to hitch and kick.
Does Skipper see how we
are trying to keep an even breath?
The lough fjord spits where summer's shift
is brimmed to seethe and slap.
His eyes have watered out of cloud.
We grip the slats.
Once parallel to the other pier,
he calls out — *Everyone off*
But docking us is swayed and slow.
He watches as we scrape and pull
at odds with our arrival.

First Time Up

How could we catch their weird? They speak so fast.
We flip the ashtrays in a borrowed car, the driver worries
where to park and we're becoming cousinly through lives
slid from under a remark. What would they expect?
Not the blue-bruised roses that we brought them by the root.

They might be out on nights we're in our beds, setting snares
in the whin that we call furze. We thought we know the island.
Theirs is colonised. Pine martens occupy the roof.
A hum of bees warms a hidden loft, the line of sparrows
stuffed to look alive. Someone must dust.

We see them reel with hands that stroke the coats
of ferrets sent down-warren. Hung in their bunks
we'll sway away the distance from that skiff, feeling
the edge of likely waters, the swelling that could drown us.
Suck of bait digging, nip of fly-tying in their riddled nails,
nest spots and the fiddle of egg swapping.

Creed

By the tap of his shoes, we know him,
by the shunt of his vowels. We groomed him
from birth to be ours. Even on days in the mountains,
he's behind us in the lull of the trees.

Tap, tap he goes, striking fear into the follicles
of young girls. Their hair shaved off, their bodies
brushed and we knew if he could,
he would cut out their tongues.

To feel his power, I was brought on a march,
to the sound of horns, a colour party, their buttons
sparkle, the gleam of the guns. Are they for us?
Are they for us really?

With a wisp of whine, we sang them a ballad
of our lost youth. They closed us down. No time
to learn a hymn re-laid by hands shot through
in the hold of prayer. It's a new divine.

They can think all things at once. We're dizzy
with spin. The store I shop in, they own.
The van that delivers is freshly sprayed.
What is their game?

Their mandate is precious, they press the mandators.
They are not insane. That shriek you hear is
an ear too close to the source. Soon they will enter
the imagination where they wait to put it out.

Hothead

He could name all these, wildflowers of the Mournes
and because there was a story to be told, he could pull
through breast and brains the way they took these names
from a distant past, a past before there rose a single god
under whom the outrage was to wage.

He would name them and the stamen of their being
stood still in the act of naming. The scent of them flew
out from his tongue, a balm to the legendary wounding.

And he would touch each petal, there, like that, between
a fat finger and a solid thumb, yet not bruise it,
but trace and lift it up as if that too would clear, would hold
the sound still in the valley and resound it out beyond,
yes, let it fly to its death in a sodden sky.

Field

for W.H.Davies

Despite the cowslips swinging their
framed yellow dottiness in the leeside
of the hedge, the land here is thistle-bound
in the main, though corncrakes, skylarks,
geese from the frozen wastes still come
as if to feed this farmer's charity —
that donkey the grandchild named again,
the hobbled pony which will never
win a ribbon; Then, I notice just how far
the hill behind has moved away in air that
shifts my eyeline to a hare running its heart
out down the median of a field that is
screaming silent in the sun.

That Water Speaks in Tongues

The trough beside the house is thick
with dashed hopes. There before brick,
before mortar, for travelling horses, stages
from their posts, its sides poured and patted
keep the mark of spade and blade, spit
in its motted pocks and fear of the ganger.

This is the drowning spot for runts of litters,
sow's disgrace squealing down the night,
when straw runs short and tempers fester envy.
Here birds fall, the souls of angels trapped
in slow-flapped deaths though no-one ventures
why in heaven's name they failed to fly.

But it's the cat, set on the aspic shelf
that stays wet to the touch. Rigor bound
with four trip-rigid legs. Cat in its drowned
death no longer Tabby, but something more dead,
more of a shock to find in the wide morning
of visitor delight than any reminder
that we know nothing yet.